Quilling

Techniques and Inspiration

Jane Jenkins

SEARCH PRESS

First published in Great Britain 2003

Search Press Limited
Wellwood, North Farm Road,
Tunbridge Wells, Kent TN2 3DR

Reprinted 2003

Text copyright © Jane Jenkins
Designs copyright © Jane Jenkins

Photographs by Charlotte de la Bédoyère,
Search Press Studios
Photographs and design copyright © Search Press Ltd 2003

ISBN 0 85532 990 4

The Publishers and author can accept no responsibility for
any consequences arising from the information, advice or
instructions given in this publication.

Readers are permitted to reproduce any of the pictures in
this book for their personal use, or for the purposes of
selling for charity, free of charge and without the prior
permission of the Publishers. Any use of the pictures for
commercial purposes is not permitted without the prior
permission of the Publishers.

Suppliers
If you have difficulty in obtaining any of the materials and
equipment mentioned in this book, then please write to the
Publishers, at the address above, for a current list of
stockists, including firms who operate a mail-order service.

> **Publisher's note**
> All the step-by-step photographs in this book feature
> the author, Jane Jenkins, demonstrating quilling. No
> models have been used.

Printed in Spain by Elkar S. Coop. Bilbao 48012

> *For Paul – this is almost as much his
> book as it is mine*

ACKNOWLEDGEMENTS

For converting my considerable apprehension into
calm, clear thinking, everyone at Search Press: a
wonderfully friendly set of experts, determined above
all things to get it right.

For never complaining, my family, who live with or
visit me. They have been forced to endure the paper,
card, glue, patterns and general quilling clutter. Their
smiling support is a constant joy.

For Lesley Davies – her understanding, reassurance
and sense of humour have kept me balanced ... mostly.

For their interest, encouragement and indulgence, my
students past and present. They have kept my feet on
the ground and made me glad to go to work
each morning.

My Quilling Guild comrades – they have ensured that
the great strides made by quilling over the past twenty
years, both in quality and variety, have been
recognised. Without that, this book could not have
come about.

Mouse on a Corn Stalk

Height: 23cm (9in)
*The mouse is made from various cone
coils and the corn from Closed Loose
Coils.*

Contents

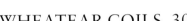

Introduction

Sometimes when I am sitting with my family in the evening and quilling while watching television or chatting, it occurs to me what a peculiar thing this is to be doing. What on earth can be the appeal in rolling, looping, twisting and curling little strips of paper? I have no simple answer, except to note that this is something I did long before I became a quiller, twenty years ago. It was always the case that, by the time I left a waiting room, the corner of my magazine was rolled, folded or crimped and, by the end of a bus journey, my ticket was manipulated beyond recognition. I am sure I am not alone in this. Give almost anyone a piece of paper and enforced idleness and they will most probably 'fiddle' in a similar way. Part of the appeal may be a certain therapeutic effect. Rather like worry beads, quilling provides a soothing, repetitive action which calms and relaxes. Unlike worry beads, basic materials are almost always near at hand. Paper is everywhere. Find a decent glue and you can produce a finished quilling in just a few minutes.

This is exactly what happened to me when I first began. I found it hard to believe that such simplicity could produce something so charming. And that, of course, is another attraction of quilling. The final result is so intriguingly lovely, which is why people who see quilling for the first time almost invariably frown and smile at the same time. 'Isn't it lovely – what is it?' The sight of the natural forms and shapes of our world, depicted in tiny spirals, curls or loops, somehow adds a whole new dimension and the result is something fascinating and delightful to look at.

Our quilling ancestors recognised this, of course, and many modern quillers find delight in knowing that they are involved in an ancient craft, adding to its history and, with the help of our modern materials, putting it to new uses.

And what a lot of uses there are! One of the most appealing things I have discovered about quilling is its versatility. Quillers create an amazing variety of pictures and plaques, models and mobiles, boxes, jewellery, decorative eggs and, of course, most popular of all, greetings cards, which say in such a personal way that you are thinking of someone.

Quillings can be simple and quick, large and elaborate, plain or colourful, cute or classy; appealing to all ages and both sexes; quilling bridges more than one generation gap and often helps and sustains in a practical way those of us with a physical or mental disability.

But the versatility of quilling is not only in the variety of finished products. It is also in the way that traditional ideas continue to be changed and developed. I enjoy nothing better than to play about with those little paper strips, developing what I know and inventing something new. If my efforts bear fruit, I have been known to stay up well into the night to finish the new creation, too excited to sleep.

As I said at the beginning – a peculiar thing to get carried away with! However, the simple fact that it is possible to sit with one's family and quill at the same time is a great point in its favour. Judging by the party atmosphere which prevails in my classes and workshops, I would say quilling is one of the great social crafts of all time.

Art Nouveau Lady

Size: 30 x 30cm (12 x 12in)

This piece features Open Coils at their simplest and their most complex. The roses are made in the Rennie Mackintosh style appropriate to the period. The body of the dress and the bird are made from Closed Loose Coils, as are the leaves.

History

Quillers working today with modern papers and glue produce work in many new and original ways. Many of the techniques we use are new, but most of them are based on old ideas seen on antique pieces in museums and stately homes. These antiques are usually from Georgian or Victorian times since quilling (also known as paper filigree or paper rollwork) was very popular among ladies of the time, who could buy their paper strips with or without gilt edges, or cut their own from the pages of books. They liked to cover boxes and especially tea caddies with quilling and there are plenty of good examples to be seen. They are easily recognisable with their usually octagonal shape, lid ring, lock and key. Charlotte Brontë quilled such a tea caddy for her friend, Ellen Nussey. George III's daughter, Elizabeth, was a quiller, and Jane Austen writes in *Sense and Sensibility* that a character 'was rolling strips for her friend Lucy Steele'.

There are also some lovely items of furniture covered entirely in quilling – the result of years of careful work.

A typical Georgian tea caddy, decorated with quilling. Strips have been handmade and some are gilt-edged, so they may have been hand-cut from the pages of a book.

Opposite

Giles Family Coat of Arms

Size: 22cm (13in) square

This quilled coat of arms, belonging to the author, dates from the eighteenth century and features strips varying from 1mm (^{1}/$_{32}$in) to 10mm (¾in) wide. All are gilded and mounted on a red velvet background, inside a 5cm (2in) deep box frame with a glass cover.

You may also be lucky enough to find a seventeenth or eighteenth century armorial plaque, since it was the pleasure of the more ambitious and skilled genteel ladies of the time to produce their family coat of arms in three-dimensional quilling, gold-edged and with the finest strips their nimble fingers could manage.

Further back in history we find ecclesiastical pieces quilled by monks and nuns to house ancient relics or decorate religious plaques.

Before this, quilling fades into the unknown, since paper decays when left unprotected. We can, therefore, only speculate about the earliest forms, which must surely have evolved from the metal and other filigree work so popular in Middle Eastern and Egyptian early civilisations.

I have little doubt, however, that the compulsion to 'fiddle' with strips of paper is not a new one. Wherever and whenever paper or a paper-like material existed, there surely existed quilling also.

Materials

Paper strips The ideal quilling strips are usually made from good quality paper of around 100gsm weight. You can buy these ready-made; the standard length is 45cm (18in) long. Standard width is 3mm ($^1/_8$in), but you can buy them in any width you choose. As well as being available in a huge range of plain colours, you can now buy some quite unusual ones. Graduated strips have a graded colour intensity along their length; Graduated Dark Centre go from white, through to deep colour and back to white again; Two-tone strips have a different colour on each side; Parchment Effect are light and pastel, Fluorescent are bright and bold. Our quilling ancestors were very fond of using gilt-edged strips and this has been taken further by modern quillers, who use gold, silver, coloured metallic and pearl-edged strips.

Sheets of paper It is sometimes easier, more economical or more effective to use coloured paper sheets to cut to your requirements. Again, choose good quality paper, around 100gsm in weight.

Glue PVA craft glue is best, suitably tacky, with a good 'grab', water-based, drying clear and non-toxic. A poor quality, watery glue will cause annoyance and frustration, so be sure to buy the best.

Applicators A fine tip applicator is not a necessity (a cocktail stick will do), but it is a very useful modern invention. A cocktail stick is also useful for moving coils around and for making Tendrils.

Mounts More often than not, you need a background for your quilling. This could be a thin card, cardboard, wood, cork, hessian or, in fact, anything to which you can get the coils to stick.

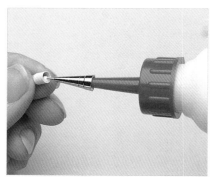

A typical quilling glue, PVA with a fine tip applicator to help you use only the minimum.

Modern papers and card provide quillers with endless options.

Opposite

Ready-cut quilling strips can be bought in any width and colour to suit the project.

A home-made quilling board made from polystyrene covered in plastic food wrap, and a quilling in progress using long bead-headed pins.

Quilling board with pins A piece of polystyrene (styrofoam) will do for this; about 15cm (6in) square and at least 2.5cm (1in) deep. Cover it in plastic food wrap, greaseproof paper or cereal packet liner but leave one edge open so that you can slide patterns underneath. Bead-headed pins are easier to hold but not the kind you use for noticeboards – these are too short.

Tweezers A variety of these can be used for different jobs; flat-ended for holding Open Coils or lengths of strip, fine-pointed straight ones for delicate work and locking tweezers for securely holding shapes.

Scissors Small, sharp, comfortable scissors are ideal for snipping, and longer ones for cutting lengths of paper. Fancy paper edgers and pinking shears are good for special effects.

Crimping machine If you want to use crimped paper, you will need a block with two small cogs, fixed so that a paper strip or two can run between them.

Ruler Any kind will do. You will not use it much.

Optional

Bulldog clip Good for gripping paper while you snip, when making Fringed Flowers.

Felt-tipped pens The wider ones for edging strips occasionally, and others for little touches.

Ink pads Again, for edging the strips. Simply pat the stamp on the finished quilling.

Needle tool For rolling paper strips – if you really must! Try to roll strips with your fingers only, if possible. You will become a far more expert quiller, more in control of your paper. Better coils can be made by using fingers only than by any tool, but if you really must use a tool, make sure it is fine, so that you can make shapes that coil right to the centre. This kind of tool can be very sharp so you need to take extra care. Children, especially, should be taught to use their fingers only.

Various dowels

Dowels Various sizes for making Ring Coils and a few other techniques. Anything from a wastepaper bin to a pencil will do – my favourite is a finger!

Corsage pin Some quillers like to roll strips around this.

Onion holder For making Wheatear Coils, if you prefer this method.

Felt-tipped pens and ink pads for edging strips.

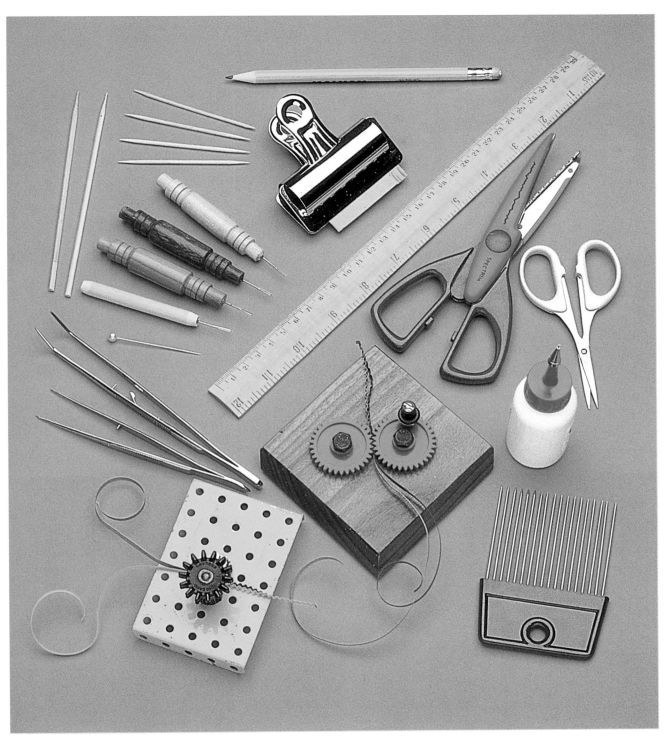

Typical quilling equipment – clockwise from bottom right: onion holder, crimping machine, tweezers, corsage pin, needle tools, skewers, cocktail sticks, bulldog clip, pencil, ruler, fancy paper edgers, scissors, glue with a fine tip applicator. Don't dash out and buy everything all at once. Buy each item when and if you need it.

11

Closed Loose Coils

This is definitely the one to start with. Easy to learn, versatile, adaptable and the most popular of all quilling techniques. Let's just be sure we get it right!

Briefly, you roll up a paper strip, release it, glue down the end and shape it to whatever is required. It's as simple as that – or is it?

Take a look at the five Teardrop-shaped Closed Loose Coils, all made from the same length strip, at the bottom of the page opposite. Which do you think is right? The answer is, they are all right. It just depends on the effect you wish to produce. But it is important that you recognise differences and that you are in complete control of your strips. A good craftsperson is able to make his or her materials do exactly what is required for the occasion.

So, for example, if your coil has a dense edge, as the three coils at bottom right have, that is fine, so long as you meant it to have one. If, on the other hand, it just happens, then your paper strip is in control, not you, so try again. Coils with dense edges are not as easy to shape, and have a different appearance. Do not be tempted to make coils the required size by preventing them opening as much as they want to. The way to regulate coil size is to regulate strip length.

In fact, it will be valuable to try making lots of coils with different appearances by changing the tension; the speed at which you roll; the way you hold the strip; how much you release it; the way you squeeze it into shape – and even the kind and weight of paper strip you use. You will find your quilling so much richer and more varied if you spend a little time experimenting, and you are so much more likely to produce 'perfect' coils more often.

However, we should not get too bogged down with producing the 'perfect' coil every time. We are, after all, meant to be enjoying this. The main thing is that you should be happy with your quilling and your coils are, in fact, what you want them to be.

Merlin

Height: 30cm (12in)

Apart from his eye (a Solid Coil), and his longest wing feathers (Wheatear Coils), the bird and branch are all made from Closed Loose Coils. To achieve a really natural appearance, I painted coloured sheets of 100gsm paper with watercolour on one side (grey on blue, brown on beige, etc.) and cut the strips by hand to the width and length I needed.

Techniques

If you are a complete beginner, practise making Closed Loose Coils using strips which are rather wider than usual – 5mm or 6mm (¼in) is good. Strips should be around 22cm (9in) in length. Just a few hints before you begin. When dividing a quilling strip, tear, rather than cut. A torn end glues down more smoothly. When starting a coil, slightly damp fingers are helpful. Only use minimum amounts of glue, perhaps using a fine tip applicator or a cocktail stick.

Now roll up your strip. People do this in different ways. As long as the result is good, it does not matter how you do it. Many quillers, for example, use a tool to roll up their strips. Some roll around a corsage pin or a cocktail stick. Here is my preferred way.

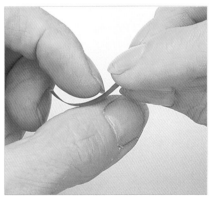

1 Use half-length strips. Scratch the end of the strip with the tip of your index finger against your thumb, to curl and soften it.

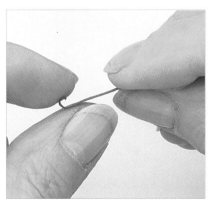

2 Bend over the very tip. Dampen your finger and thumb first if that is helpful.

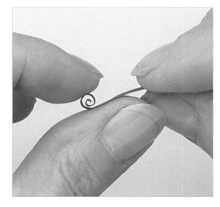

3 Rub your finger along your thumb and feel the strip roll between them.

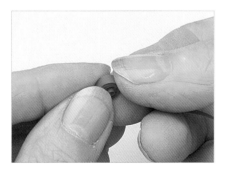

4 Relax. Let the strip go. Turn the coil sideways and roll as you would a tiny tape measure.

5 As soon as you get to the end, let the coil go completely. It will spring open.

6 Glue down the end just where it wants to lie. You want a regular, even coil all the way from centre to edge, so do not pull the end before gluing it down.

7 You can use the coil in this shape (round) or squeeze it into many others: teardrops, eye shapes, leaf shapes, squares, triangles etc. – see page 13.

Try **Double Rolling:**

1 Glue two strips together at their tip.

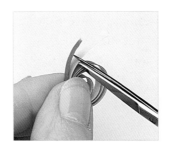

2 Roll, release and cut the inside strip a little shorter before gluing down.

End-to-end Rolling is achieved by gluing two strips together end-to-end, creating a coil with a different colour towards its centre.

Eccentric Coils are made by holding the centre of the coil to the edge. Hold the edges together with tweezers and rub glue into the edges of the strips. Allow to dry before releasing.

Try these **Charles Rennie Mackintosh** style roses.

1 Glue two strips together at their tips. Instead of rolling, bend, and continue in a series of bends along the full length, rolling tightly.

2 Release the oval shaped coil and coax it to open.

3 Glue down the strip ends. The resulting rose is uncannily like some of Mackintosh's.

Art Nouveau Iris

I have to admit to being a great fan of Art Nouveau. The flowing, almost mobile lines, especially when placed alongside the strictly vertical and horizontal, create a counterplay of the graceful and the solid, which is delightful to behold.

My editor gave me the inspiration for this beautiful, curvy and symmetrical Iris, adapted to a quilled design. It is made entirely from Closed Loose Coils of various shapes and sizes and includes some special variations, Double Rolling, End-to-End Rolling and an Eccentric Coil.

Let us start with that Eccentric Coil because it goes right at the centre and we might as well get the hardest bit over with first!

The pattern for this project is on page 74.

The pattern for this project is on page 74.

You will need

Standard length, 3mm (¹/₈in) wide quilling strips: eight purple, one mauve, one pale yellow, nine black, four lilac, seven sage
One pale yellow and one bright yellow strip, 2mm or 1.5mm (¹/₁₆in) wide
Glue
Tweezers
Cream mount 20 x 26cm (8 x 10in)
Dowel (lipstick)
Fine scissors

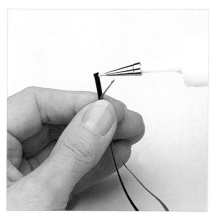

1 Glue two full-length strips, one black and one purple, together at their tips.

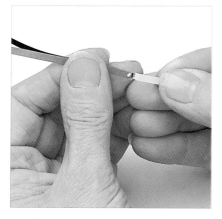

2 Glue a quarter-length (11cm/ 4½in) pale yellow strip to the glued end of the other two.

3 Roll up, beginning at the pale yellow end, and with the purple on the outside of the coil.

4 Release the coil and cut the black strip slightly shorter than the purple one. Glue down the end of the purple strip just where it wants to lie.

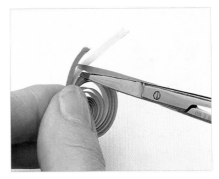

5 Now you need to turn it into an Eccentric Coil, using either your quilling board and pins or locking tweezers to hold the centre of the coil to the edge. Rub some glue on the edges of the strips where they are being held together. Allow glue to dry thoroughly before releasing.

Note
Do not pull the strip round to glue it.

6 Mark the centre of your mount by making two diagonals from corner to corner. Put a few tiny dots of glue on the back of your Eccentric, Double Rolled, End-to-End Closed Loose Coil (phew!) and glue it dead centre of the mount.

7 Glue two full-length (45cm/ 18in) strips, one purple and one lilac, together at their tips and Double Roll them with the purple on the outside. Cut the lilac strip a little shorter and glue down the end of the purple strip.

8 Squeeze and press this Double Rolled Coil into a curved Teardrop shape. Pinch the curved ends slightly. You will need two of these for the 'horned' petals at the top of the flower.

9 Repeat Step 7 but shape the resulting coil into a crescent, using a dowel of some kind (I used a lipstick). Again, you will need two, of course.

10 Glue the four coils to the background, being careful to place them symmetrically.

11 Make the tiny petals in the main flower using a quarter-length mauve strip for each Closed Loose Coil. For the leaves, make seven Closed Loose Coils using one sage green strip for each. Shape and glue them down following the pattern on page 74. Make the lower buds, amongst the leaves, by Double Rolling a quarter purple and a quarter black strips together. The higher buds are made with one purple strip each. Glue all these parts down as shown.

12 Make a small coil for the centre of the flower using an eighth of a 3mm (1/8in) pale yellow strip and glue it directly on to the mount. Then make the tiny yellow coils for the second layer using nine one-sixteenth-length 2mm or 1.5mm ($^1/_{16}$in) wide paper strips in pale yellow and bright yellow. Glue these nine on top, as shown in the pattern.

13 For the black Japanese-style border, use quarter-length black strips to make Closed Loose Coils and shape them into sixteen squares as shown.

The finished Art Nouveau Iris
12 x 17.5cm (4¾ x 7in)

Celtic Knot

Size: 155 x 120mm (6 x 4¾in)

A mix of the old and the new, this quilling was inspired by the ever-popular designs of the ancients. However, it was quilled using a very modern innovation: blue and red metallic-edged strips, to give it an exotic shine.

Opposite

Quilled Tribute to Charles Rennie Mackintosh

Size: 210 x 297mm (8¼ x 11¾in)

What can I say about the great C. R. M.? His work, so uniquely recognisable, inspires many artists/craftworkers in jewellery, wood, interior design, embroidery, stained glass and fashion, to mention just a few. Quilling, also, is an ideal medium to create 'Toshie'-style designs, so here is my tribute.

I made the big Ring Coils around saucepans of different sizes. The leaves are black-edged Closed Loose Coils, the flowers are made in black using the technique described on page 15, with Closed Loose Coils slotted in.

Open Coils

The thing about Open Coils is that they look best if they are 'open'. This may sound a rather obvious statement but it is a mistake often made that the coil produced is so similar in appearance to that of a Closed Loose Coil as to be a rather pointless exercise. If we take a good look at the wrought-iron work on gates and fences, in churches and surrounding stately homes, the beautiful effect is created as much by the space between the ironwork as it is by the filigree shapes themselves. This is the effect we need to create with our paper strips, keeping in mind that decorative metalwork was probably the earliest inspiration for paper filigree.

The charm of Open Coils is their light and delicate appearance. Complete quillings may be made entirely from Open Coils but, generally, they are used in conjunction with denser and more solid coils to create contrast.

Opposite

Examples of Open Coils

Libra

Height: 110mm (4¼in)
Open Coils with their typical wrought-iron appearance. This zodiac design is made from strips with a gilded edge.

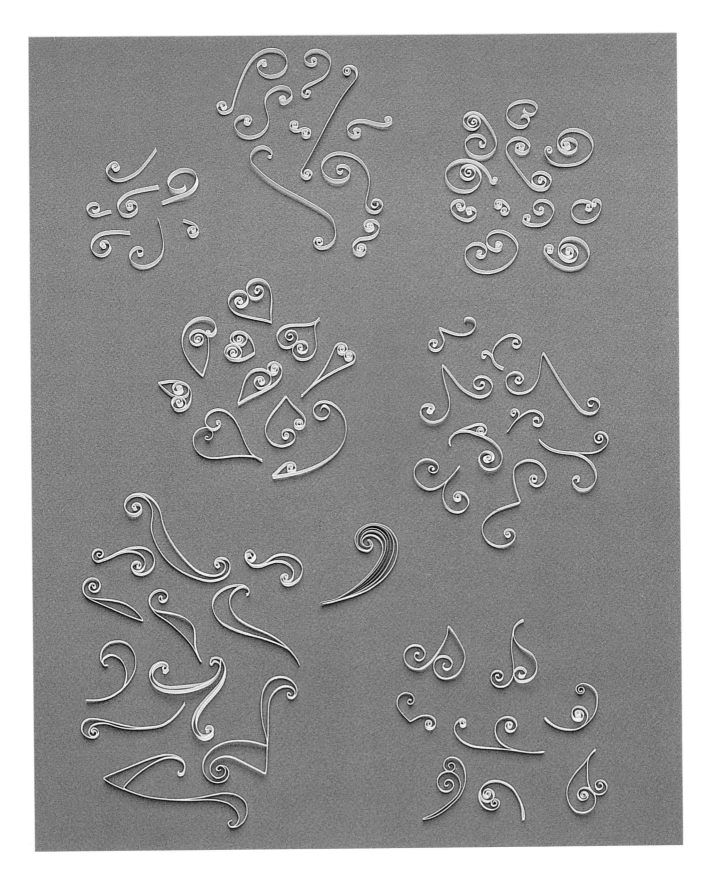

Techniques

The most effective and controllable way to make really elegant Open Coils is to manipulate the paper strips between finger and thumb. In the same way as you begin a Closed Loose Coil, scratching and curling the strip end means that you can roll and unroll, curve and straighten, increase and decrease the size of coil, thus creating exactly the Open Coil you want.

Again, it is a good idea to take time to practise. Use wider strips than standard: 5mm or 6mm (¼in) is good and strip lengths should be 11cm (4½in) – a quarter of a standard length strip. Here are the basic shapes; see how many variations you can make.

Simple – using an eighth-length strip

Antennae, using a quarter-length strip

Heart, using a quarter-length strip

Cherries

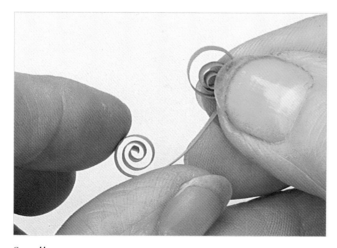

Scroll

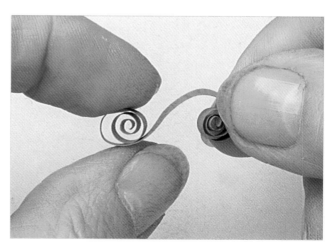

'S'

Double Open Coil

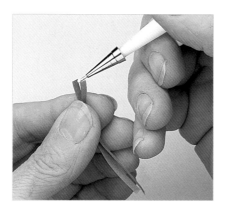

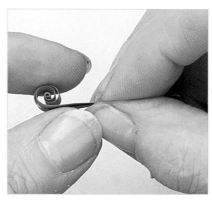

1 Glue two eighth-length strips together at their tip.

2 Roll the glued end a little.

3 Slide the two apart. Now you have a Double Open Coil. Glue the other ends to fix in place.

Multi-strip Open Coil

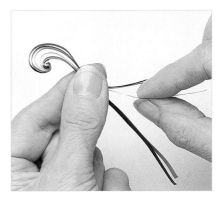

1 To make a Multi-strip Open Coil, glue several strips together at their tip.

2 Roll the end a little.

3 Hold the strips sideways and separate them by pulling or pushing each loose end individually.

4 Fix the ends in place with glue.

Victorian Fan

Filigree quilling is undeniably reminiscent of lace and, to my mind, black lace is particularly striking. I had, therefore, made several attempts at a black lace fan before it occurred to me to make one in this way. A very strong structure combines with a delicate appearance to make a full-sized fan, with no real need for a fixed background. The pattern for this project is on page 75.

You will need

Eighty standard length, 3mm (¹⁄₈in) wide black strips; more for decoration if desired
Nine paper squares, 11cm (4¼in)
Quilling board and pins
Tweezers

1 Cut nine squares of sides approximately 11cm (4½in). Start by scratching the corner of each square. Then make them into spills by rolling them diagonally across as tightly as possible.

2 Glue these to each other and press so that they open naturally into 'V' shapes. Nine of these shapes will make a complete semicircle.

Each section of the fan is made in the same way so we will make one complete section, which you can repeat.

3 Using half-length (22cm/9in) strips, make a five-petal flower from Closed Loose Coils (see pages 12–15).

4 Roll a half-length (22cm/9in) strip as tightly as possible. Do not allow it to uncoil. Glue down the end and place this Solid Coil on top of your flower to make a good, strong centre.

5 Glue the flower to the spines of the fan where they fit best, probably about two-thirds of the way up. Fix the pieces in place with pins.

6 Use a half-length (22cm/9in) strip and your finger, or whatever is the right size dowel, to make three Ring Coils. These should fit just above your flowers. Top them with a Solid Coil, made from a full-length (45cm/18in) strip. For Ring Coils and Solid Coils see the Tight Coils chapter on page 48.

7 Two leaf-shaped Closed Loose Coils go just below the flower, and Teardrop shapes are tucked right in at the base. Use full-length (45cm/18in) strips.

8 Make a symmetrical Antennae Open Coil from a quarter-length (11cm/4½in) strip and glue it below the leaf shapes.

9 Make two Open Coil Cherries and place them at the top of your fan section.

10 Make two Open Coil Modified Heart shapes and place them at the top of your fan's section as shown. Complete all the other sections of the fan in the same way.

Note

You can add more Closed Loose Coil shapes to the spine of your fan to decorate it.

The finished Victorian Fan project, which is 300 x 150mm (12 x 6in). The black, lacy design shows off Open Coils at their best, with the denser Tight Coils and Closed Loose Coils.

Chinese Fish

Size: 240 x 180mm (9½ x 7¼in)

Open Coils make fabulous border designs – if you can get them all to look uniform!

The tail and fins of this exotic fish are of course Multi-strip Open Coils, but not so obviously, the 'filling quilling' inside the fish itself also consists of Open Coils. They are in fact 'S' shapes, quicker and easier than Closed Loose Coils and more adaptable for pushing into tiny areas where necessary.

29

Wheatear Coils

There are three good reasons for choosing the Wheatear Coil technique in your quilling. The first is for strength. Each loop is fixed in place with glue so that free-standing quillings, mobiles, ear-rings and Christmas tree decorations, where we need to be sure that coil centres will not fall out, can be made with confidence.

A second good quality of a Wheatear Coil is that it can be made much bigger or longer than the Closed Loose Coil. The leaves of some flowers, for example, are very tall, so a Wheatear Coil fits the bill. Similarly, flower stalks, made from very few, long loops, look so much better than a single piece of paper strip.

However, the main quality that makes us choose a Wheatear Coil over other techniques is simply its appearance. Those lovely, regular loops provide diversity in a quilling. So, for example in a flower arrangement, the introduction of petals made from Wheatears will provide contrast and make the whole thing more interesting.

Daffodils

Height: 15cm (6in)

The flowers themselves are made from Closed Loose Coils but the long leaves and stalks look best made from Wheatears.

Examples of Wheatear Coils with variations

Techniques

Wheatear Coils made using your fingers only require a great deal of handling and gluing. It is, therefore, rather easy to get into a sticky mess!

Remember, good quality PVA glue requires only a little time rather than a huge blob in order to adhere efficiently. Practise with strips rather wider than standard: 5mm or 6mm (¼in) is good. When you feel ready, you can move over to the usual 3mm (⅛in).

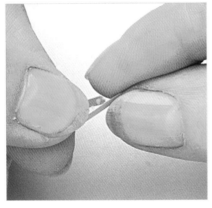

1 Make a small loop in the end of a strip and glue it in place.

2 Bring the strip over and make a slightly larger loop.

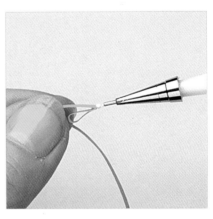

3 Hold the loops sideways while you put a tiny drop of glue on the pointed end.

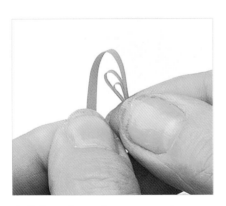

4 Bring the strip over again and repeat.

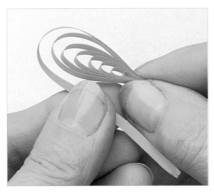

5 Continue to loop until the Wheatear Coil is as big as you want it to be. If necessary, add more strip at the pointed end.

6 An alternative way to make Wheatears is to use an onion holder.

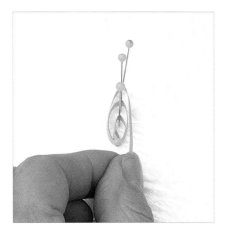

7 You can also use a quilling board and pins.

8 Wheatears may be made with two or more strips, and loops do not have to be equally spaced.

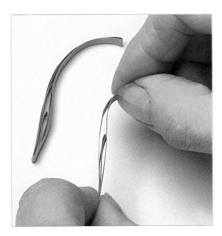

9 The further apart you make the loops, the longer and thinner the Wheatear. Two large loops, pressed and scratched flat, make an excellent flower stalk.

10 A variation on the Wheatear Coil can be made by using a dowel of some kind, a finger or a pencil perhaps, so that the result is round rather than teardrop-shaped.

Tulips

I love the way tulip flowers reach for the sky while their leaves bend in all directions, especially when they are bunched in a vase. Wheatear Coils are perfect for making those long, narrow leaves which form so much of the interest in this project. Make them in at least three different greens, using 3mm ($^1/8$in) wide strips throughout the first layer. The pattern for this project is on page 76.

You will need

Standard length, 3mm ($^1/8$in) wide strips: three blue; twenty in two or three different greens; four in two or three different reds
Glue
Mount: 18 x 20cm (7 x 8in)

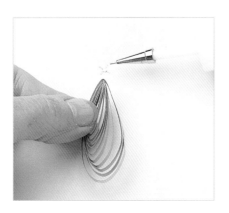

1 Make a Wheatear Coil from blue strips (Two-tone strips look particularly good). Loops need to be close together and the final teardrop shape should measure about 5cm (2in). Glue this to your background with tiny drops of glue so that the point is exactly central.

2 Make a tapered rectangular Closed Loose Coil from a half-length (11cm/4½in) Two-tone blue strip to complete the vase.

3 Make five tulip flowers in shades of red from one, two or three Closed Loose Coils. Larger petals are made from half-length strips, smaller ones from quarter-length, and the tiny petal in the top flower from an eighth-length strip. Glue the flowers in place, either like mine or in an arrangement of your own. Note that the tips of the tallest flower should be at least 6cm (3½in) above the top of the vase.

The finished Tulips project
Height: 130cm (3in)

4 Now make the leaves. You will need lots of Wheatears, some of which you can bend. Follow my pattern or make your own arrangement. Add a second layer of leaves on top of the first. Make five more green Wheatears, this time using 1.5 or 2mm ($^1/_{16}$in) wide strips. The big leaf which comes down over the top of the vase is a Closed Loose Coil made from two full lengths, double-rolled and shaped as a Teardrop. Again, use narrower strips if possible.

Wheatear Flowers

297 x 210 (11¾ x 8¼in)

To achieve this bright and bold appearance, I used graduated colour strips which are white at one end and gradually deepen to a strong colour at the other.

Peacock in a Bower

Height: 230mm (9in)
In contrast, the whole of this design was
made in cream-coloured strips on a cream
background.

Alternate Side Looping

My favourite technique! It looks great, is so easy to do and has very many uses and variations, which means it can be both delicate and strong. Alternate Side Looping is, therefore, an excellent choice for many situations.

Everything I said in praise of Wheatear Coils can be applied to Alternate Side Looping. Like Wheatears, the main reason quillers use it is to add interest and contrast to a quilling. Alternate Side Looping has the added advantage of being, in my opinion, the most adaptable technique of all, more so, even, than the ever popular Closed Loose Coil. I spend a great deal of time experimenting or 'playing' with quilling strips to see what happens and whether the result is useful to quillers. I think it is safe to say I have had more success with Alternate Side Looping than anything else. So, when you have learned the basics, have a go at experimenting yourself. You never know what might emerge.

Wedding Flowers

Width: 170mm (6½in)

This pastel arrangement is made almost entirely of Alternate Side Looping variations.

Examples of Alternate Side Looping and variations

Techniques

In describing the Alternate Side Looping technique, I discover I have something of a basic terminology problem. Unlike the techniques described so far, we are not rolling or taking the paper strip around in one direction. This means that the result cannot, by any stretch of the imagination be called a 'coil'. Sometimes the term 'Husking' is used to describe basic Alternate Side Looping so I have decided for the sake of clarity to use that term for all the results of Alternate Side Looping, even those which are very complicated, and look nothing like the basic Husking.

As usual, practising with 5mm or 6mm (¼in) wide strips is easier for a complete beginner.

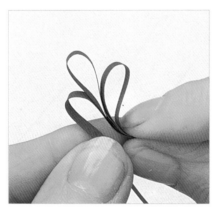

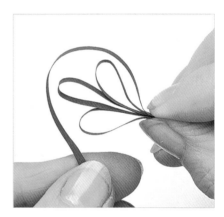

1 Make a loop about 3cm (1¼in) tall. It is not necessary to put glue on the strip end but you could if it helps. Hold this loop sideways and make a second loop by its side, a little smaller than Loop 1.

2 Bring the strip to the other side of Loop 1 and then make a third loop about the same size as Loop 2.

3 Take the strip up and over all three loops. This is called the Enclosing Loop.

4 Pull the Enclosing Loop so that it fits snugly over the ends of the other loops and cut off excess strip. Glue down the end. This is a simple 'Three Loop Husking'.

The finished husking

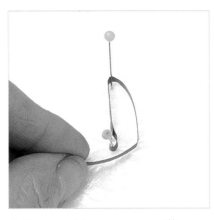

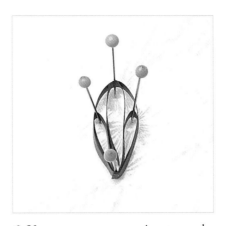

5 You could use your quilling board and pins to make simple Huskings. Begin by making a tiny loop in the end of the strip, through which to put your anchor pin.

6 You can now use pins to make your loops alternately, right and left, as before. This method is particularly good when a design requires symmetry.

7 Of course, you can make Huskings with any number of loops and you can vary their length.

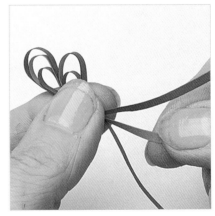

8 Usually, the first loop(s) are the tallest but it is possible to make them the smallest and, also, to make random sizes. They will be held snugly together by the final Enclosing Loop.

9 You don't have to have an Enclosing Loop at all but this style of Husking needs a tiny dot of glue at the anchor point every time the strip goes past it.

10 You can make Huskings using more than one strip together. Each time you make a loop, hold it sideways and pull each strip to separate it from its neighbour.

Butterfly

Originally, these butterflies were made with no background. The wings were glued to each other, then to the butterfly body, and then the whole was perched on a quilled pencil end or a stick included in a flower arrangement. The whole quilling was then treated with spray varnish for protection.

However, the butterflies are more clearly visible on a mount of some kind. They may be used on a greetings card or a wooden plaque.

To make a symmetrical butterfly, you need to use a quilling board and pins. The pattern for this project is on page 77.

You will need

Standard strips, 3mm (¹/₈in) wide: thirteen in bright colours, one black
White paper to trace pattern on to
Quilling board and pins
Fine scissors
Wooden box, 11cm (4½in) in diameter, or other mount

1 Trace Wing A onto a piece of white paper and put it onto a quilling board beneath the plastic food wrap.

2 Make a tiny loop in the end of a quilling strip (Two-tone strips look great) and push the anchor pin through it and into the board. Lean the pin towards you a little.

3 Take the strip around pin 1, which should lean slightly away from you, and then down again to the anchor point.

4 Bring the strip up the left-hand side and then put pin 2 in position.

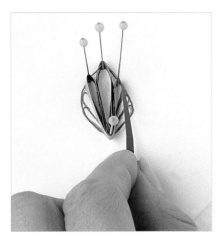

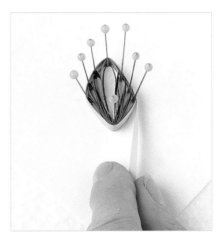

5 Bring the strip back down to the anchor point and up around pin 3.

6 Continue with Alternate Side Looping until you have used all the points. Cut off any excess strip and glue down the ends. Add another strip in a different colour and take it all the way around. Pull it snugly against the pins.

7 Glue at the anchor point and then take the strip around twice more, gluing a little as you go. Cut off excess strip and glue down the end.

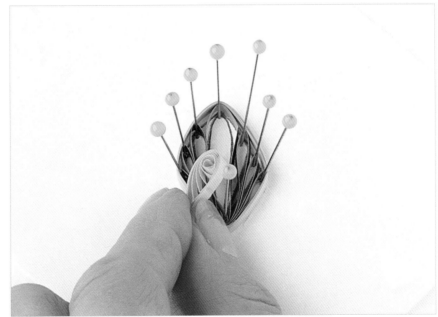

8 Make a Closed Loose Coil from a half-length (22cm/9in) strip and shape it into a long, thin Teardrop. Put a tiny dot of glue on either side and slot it into the central loop, using either fingers or tweezers. Repeat the whole Husking for a second lower wing.

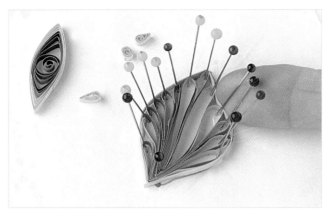

9 Make the upper wings in the same way, using the Wing B pattern as a guide. You will probably need to put a dot of glue on the tips of the loops before you make the Enclosing Loop. Hold it in place as the glue dries. Make an End-to-End rolled Closed Loose Coil using two half-length strips in contrasting colours. Make three tiny Teardrop-shaped Closed Loose Coils from a sixteenth of a strip each.

10 Glue the extra Closed Loose Coils inside the loops of the upper wings as shown. Remove the pins from the board very carefully. Glue each upper wing to a lower one as shown above.

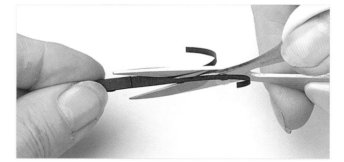

12 Glue this into position and, to make the antennae, cut the remaining strip in half along its length, rolling the ends a little.

11 To make the body, roll up a half-length (22cm/9in) black strip but stop rolling when about 5cm (2in) is remaining. Release the coil and squeeze it into an Eye shape.

13 Glue the wings to the body and the whole to your background.

The finished Butterfly project mounted on a wooden box, 11cm (4½in) in diameter. Spray with aerosol varnish to strengthen and protect your work.

Fluorescent Butterflies

Size: 225 x 290mm (9 x 11½in)

Fluorescent quilling strips – not for the faint-hearted! A black background accentuates their effect, and perhaps we should not be too concerned – after all, somewhere in nature there are sure to be butterflies even brighter. Alternate Side Looping is the perfect technique for insect wings, and you can add as little or as much extra quilling as you like to decorate them.

Opposite

Fantasy Flowers

Size: 215 x 290mm (8½ x 11½in)

The possible variations of the Alternate Side Looping technique are almost endless, so experiment, and when you find one that looks good, make four or five more and use them for the petals of a fantasy flower arrangement.

Tight Coils

I wonder if I have already said that quilling is the best craft in the world. If so, I am happy to say it again. One of the main reasons for this is that quilling can be used for such a wide variety of objects. Tight Coils prove this point perfectly because, with them, we can create not only valuable interest and contrast to a quilling but also a whole new dimension – modelling. Some quillers become so interested in this aspect of their craft that they do very little else and, since characters both big and small, comic and serious, cute, fantastical and historical abound, there seems no reason they should ever be short of a subject. Tight Coils also make excellent flower centres, free-standing pots and containers, thimbles, spinning tops, piggy banks and round boxes and lids. Did I say quilling was the best craft in the world?

Wizard and Friends

Height: 350mm (14in)

This character was great fun to make. I used 5mm (¾in) wide silver-sided strips for his robe and sleeves. Pushing and pressing such huge Tight Solid Coils into cone shapes was no easy task. However, by comparison, his beard was a doddle – 1mm (¹/₃₂ in) wide strips straight from the pack!

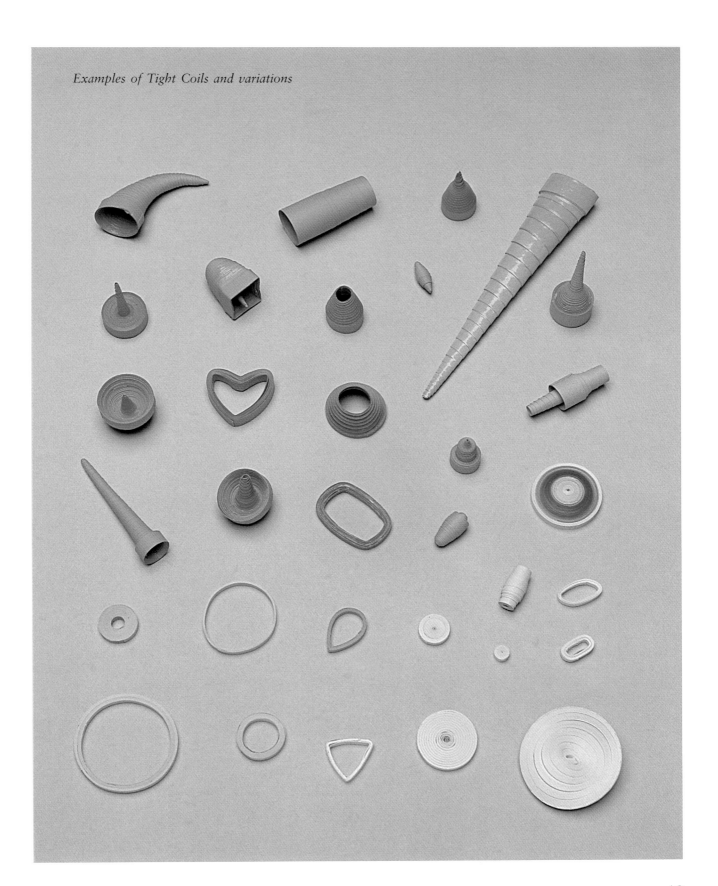

Techniques

When seen individually and unadorned, Tight Coils look most uninteresting. It is only when we see what can be done with them that their true value emerges and whole new horizons open up. There are two kinds of Tight Coils: Ring Coils and Solid Coils. Both are strong and functional.

Ring Coils can be made around a dowel of some kind: your finger, a pencil, a lipstick, a film container, a jam jar – almost anything – it does not even have to be round.

Basic Solid Coils make discs with little or no hole at the centre. These Solid Coils may also be pushed or worked into Cup or Cone Coils, which facilitate bigger modelling.

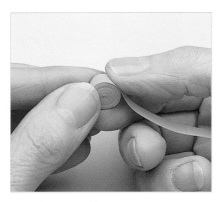

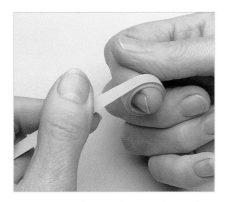

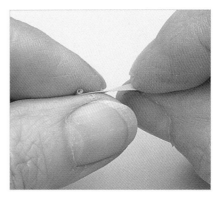

1 Take a quilling strip, any length, any width, roll it up as tightly as possible and glue down the end. This is a simple Tight Coil. Use less strip for smaller coils, add extra strips for larger ones.

2 Ring Coils can be made with or without a dowel. Simply glue the strip's end (torn is best) and form a circle or other shape. Roll tightly and glue down the end. Round Ring Coils may be shaped a little where necessary.

3 To make the perfect Solid Coil with no hole at the centre, you need to work at the strip end before you roll. Scratch and roll as you would a Closed Loose Coil but use much more pressure and do not let go. We are aiming for no hole at the centre, so I usually begin my coil and then check its centre by holding it up to the light.

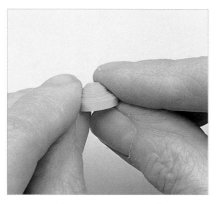

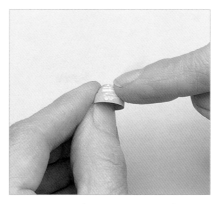

4 To make a Cup Coil, first make a Solid Coil from 3mm (¹/₈in) wide paper. Try using two full lengths. Push the coil gently into a cup shape. If it collapses, you are pushing too hard or not rolling tightly enough.

5 Use your finger to coat the inside or the outside (depending on whether or not you want a shiny finish) with PVA glue. Cup Coils may be shaped a little if required.

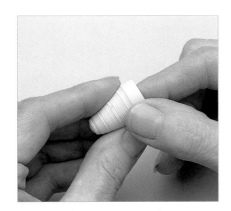

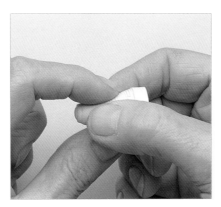

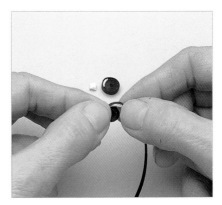

6 To make a Cone Coil, use 5mm or 6mm (¼in) strips and roll three, adding one after the other. Gently and gradually push and press the coil into a cone or use the Marycooze method described in step 7.

7 The Marycooze method involves first pushing the Solid Coil a little and then pressing alternately with the finger and thumb of each hand. Magically, the Solid Coil grows into a Cone Coil.

8 If we are quilling an animal, bird or figure, eyes with highlights add a touch of realism. Use 3mm (¹/₈in) strips. Roll a tiny piece of white strip, 2.5cm (1in) long. Release it, squash it completely flat and put it to one side. Roll a full-length black strip as tightly as possible, with no hole at the centre. Stop rolling but hold tight when a quarter of the strip remains. Incorporate the white coil. Continue to roll and glue down the end.

Foxgloves

You've got to hand it to foxgloves – they are one of Nature's success stories, perfectly designed to fit the average bumble-bee; beautiful to look at along a garden wall and able to survive almost any conditions our fickle June weather will supply.

This design makes use of tiny Cone Coils and is very three-dimensional, so if you make it into a greetings card and send it by post, you will have to wrap it in lots of padding or make or find a little box. The pattern for this project is on page 78.

You will need

*Six standard length, 3mm
(^{1}/$_8$in) wide strips in two or
three greens*
*Six 5–6mm (¼in) wide pink
Graduated Dark Centre strips*
*One 5.5mm (2¼in) square of
green tissue paper*
Fine purple felt-tipped pen
Pencil
Fine scissors
Fine tweezers
Glue
Oval mount 10cm (4in) high

1 Make a spill (see page 26) from the green tissue paper and stick down the end as shown. This will be the stalk of the foxglove.

2 Use your green strips to make the first layer of leaves from shaped Closed Loose Coils. Use half-length strips for the largest leaves at the bottom, quarter-length for the slightly smaller ones just above these, an eighth of a strip for each of the eight leaves that go up the length of the stalk, and a sixteenth of a strip for each of the three small leaves at the top. Make two more leaves for a second layer, one from a quarter- and one from a half-length strip Closed Loose Coil.

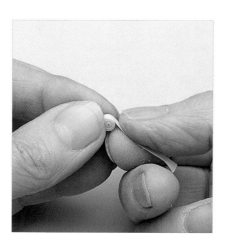

3 Use your pink Graduated Dark Centre strips for the flowers. These strips are generally shorter than average (about 32cm/14in long). Cut four of them in half. Use seven of the halves to make flowers. For each one, roll tightly, starting at the dark end. Glue down the end.

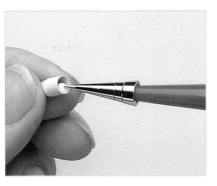

4 Push a coil onto a pencil point to form a Cone Coil.

5 Coat the inside of the coil with glue and allow to dry.

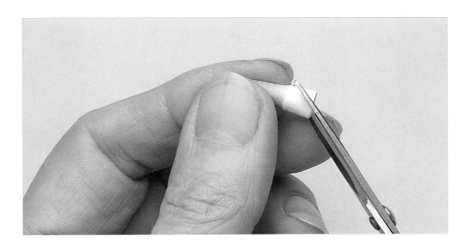

6 Use a pair of very sharp scissors to cut the mouth of the coil at a slight angle.

7 Shape, glue and cut all seven flowers in the same way. A few dots made with a fine purple felt tip pen give an authentic look to the foxgloves.

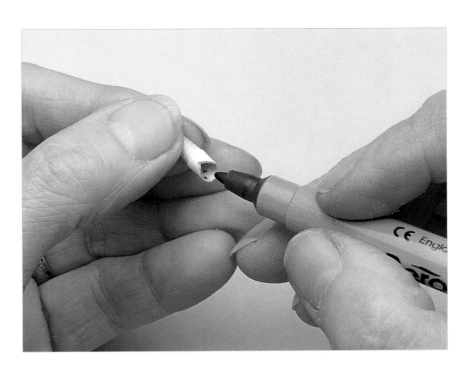

8 Arrange the foxglove's stalk and the first layer of leaves, and stick them down as shown. Stick the second layer of leaves on top of the first. Now glue your first seven flowers onto this leafy background, beginning at the bottom and allowing them to overlap as you go up the stalk.

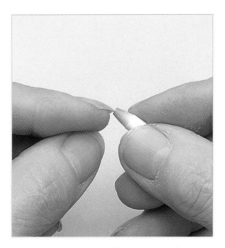

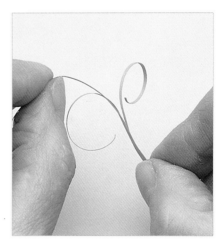

9 Cut another of your pink Graduated Dark Centre strips in half and make it into two more flowers as before. However, these flowers need to be a little smaller so, before you glue them inside, push the point back down about half way to shorten them. Add them to your foxglove stalk, above the larger flowers.

10 Cut one more of these pink strips into quarters. Take three of these quarters and make three flowers in the same way. They will, of course, be tiny. Glue them to the top of the foxglove stalk.

11 Cut an eighth of a length of one of your green strips. Cut in half along its length, almost to the end. If you are feeling brave enough, you might manage two cuts (into thirds). Scratch and curl these to make wispy foliage, and glue on to the design. Make another for the other side of the foxglove stalk, and glue on as shown.

54

The finished Foxgloves project
Height: 100mm (4in)

Flower Lady

Height: 100mm (4in)

Making miniature models is a favourite way of quilling for many people. The possibilities are, of course, endless. Solid Coils, Cup Coils and Cone Coils are used here to make the figures, the flower buckets and trays. The tiny flowers are the product of careful, clean and nimble fingers, combined with hours of work. Despite being offered a free bluebell, this little girl seems more interested in the poodle, whose fluffy coat is made from Pom-poms (see page 60).

Boxes

The diameter of the pink box is 60mm (2in). Decorating wooden boxes is popular with quillers, but these boxes go one step further: they are made entirely from quilling. Their lids are Cone Coils, their bases are Solid Coils and their sides are Ring Coils. Decoration is, of course, anything you want to make it. Treating with spray varnish will protect and strengthen your work.

Fringed Flowers

Although only a very few Fringed Flowers appear in historical quilled pieces (possibly because they are rather unconventional in appearance), they are a great example of the way quillers have taken an old idea and, using modern materials, developed it in a multitude of ways to suit our twenty-first century tastes.

Fringed Flowers have such popular appeal that even non-quillers usually warm to them, and because they are so instantly successful, they are especially loved by children. The technique is not solely used for making flowers. Animals and birds also work well, along with Santa's beard, Christmas trees and fir cones.

Fringed Flowers could be classed as a type of Solid Coil, but they are now so various and the skill of fringing so accepted as a part of our craft that they deserve a chapter to themselves.

Opposite

Examples of Fringed Flowers and variations

Fringed Flower Basket

Size: 275 x 195mm (11 x 7½in)

A very modern quilling using newly invented variations and techniques. My flower arranging friends give me lots of tips – one is to make the colours of the container match or complement the flowers.

Techniques

There are two basic kinds of Fringed Flowers from which all the variations stem. One is Pom-poms and the other is 'true' Fringed Flowers, which are made with a centre. Both are made by rolling a fringed length of paper – generally rather wider than usual. You may find, as I do, that cutting your own strips from an A4 or foolscap sheet gives you more versatility in the way you cut them. This easy-going technique will disguise an imperfect strip edge so you may cut with long scissors, as long as they are good and sharp. You are also going to need a fine, sharp, comfortable pair of scissors for fringing. As usual, a little time spent practising will pay dividends and soon you will join the rest of us, competing to see who can produce the finest fringe.

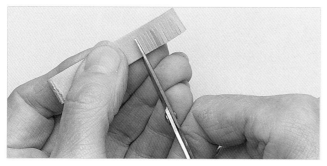

1 Use a 10mm or 12mm (½in) wide strip to practise these basic Fringed Flowers. Take a half-length (22cm/9in) strip and fold it into quarters. This is simply because the average pair of fine, sharp scissors can cut through four layers of paper comfortably. Hold the folded strip in your fingers and fringe it as finely as possible up to 3mm (⅛in) from the edge.

2 You can also hold the strip together with a bulldog clip along its very edge, as above.

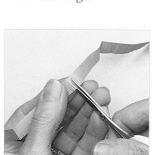

3 Open up the strip and give a little attention to the folds – they may need extra snipping.

4 Roll up the strip – it doesn't have to be super-tight – and glue down the end.

5 Spread the fringes wide with your thumbs and press them right down. The result is a simple Pom-pom, used as often for a flower centre as for the flower itself.

6 To make a 'true' Fringed Flower with a centre, first make a Solid Coil from a 3mm (⅛in) wide full-length strip. Fringe a 10mm (³⁄₈in) wide strip as before and glue it to the Solid Coil.

7 Roll up and glue down the end. Spread the fringes.

8 If you use sheets of good quality paper rather than quilling strips, you will find that you can create a greater variety of petals. For example, fancy paper edgers make petals with realistic ragged tips.

9 Another variation can be created by sloping one side of the strip. Try 15mm (⁵/₈in) down to 5mm or 6mm (³/₈in) along a 21cm (8 ¼in) length. Fold in half. Fringe the sloped side and roll from the narrow end.

10 Stick the sloped, fringed strip to a flower centre. Roll, glue down the end and spread out the petals as usual.

11 Try gluing different widths, lengths and colours end to end.

 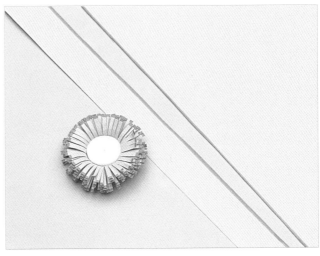

12 Double Rolling creates yet another variation. Here, light and dark purple have been used.

13 Fold a 2cm (¾in) wide strip, 21cm (8¼in) long in half along its length. Fringe the folded edge at an angle. Roll in the same direction as the cuts. Glue down the end. You will not need to spread these fringes – they do it themselves.

14 Measure 1cm (about ³/₈in) in from the edge of your paper and draw a line with a thick felt-tip pen. Cut down the middle of this line so that, when you fringe, the flower petals created will have coloured tips.

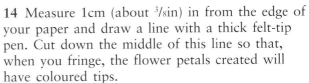

15 You can get a similar effect by patting the fringes onto a stamp pad before you spread them.

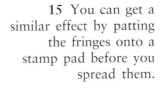 

Sunflowers

Both my mother and my mother-in-law are expert gardeners (whatever happened to me, I wonder?) and the beautiful products of their green fingers inspired me to find ways of producing Fringed Flowers which actually look like the real thing. Seed packets and gardening catalogues provided reference pictures which led, inevitably, to many happy hours attempting to reproduce Helichrysum, Centaurea, Calendula and many more. The most popular of these efforts, predictably, turns out to be the delightful Helianthus, or Sunflower, so I have made this trio for you to try. Try to make sure that you use good quality paper for the pot – around 100gsm is best. Lighter or heavier paper will roll differently. The pattern for this project is on page 79.

You will need

Ten standard length, 2mm (1/16in) wide green strips

Six 7mm (5/16in) wide, 21cm (8¼in) long strips: three each of two different shades of brown

Three 2cm (¾in) wide, 11cm (4½in) long yellow strips

Three 6cm (2in) squares of green paper

Two terracotta strips, one 1.5cm (5/8in) wide, 29cm (11½in) long; one 4.5cm (1¾in) wide, 19.5cm (7¾in) long

Fine scissors

Glue

Greetings card: 10.5 x 21cm (4 x 8¼in)

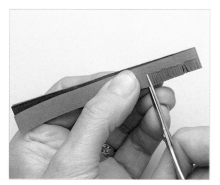

1 Take two of the 7mm (5/16in) strips in different shades of brown. Fold them in half together to make fringing quicker, and finely fringe across half their width. Roll them up together and glue down the ends.

2 Take one of the 10mm (3/8in) brown strips. Fringe as before and glue to the other two. Roll up and glue down the end.

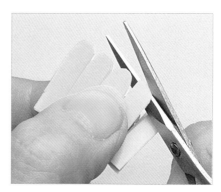

3 Take a 2cm (¾in) yellow strip. Fold twice and cut fringes coarsely about 5mm (less than ¼in) apart and up to 3mm (1/8in) from the edge of the strip. Cut the ends of the fringes into curved shapes to make them look like rounded petals.

62

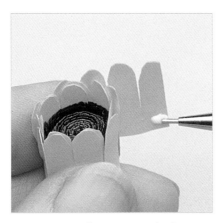

4 Open up the strip and glue it to the brown flower centre. Roll and glue down the end.

5 Open up the yellow petals very wide. Spread the longer brown fringes a little and the shorter ones a little less. Make two more flowers in exactly the same way.

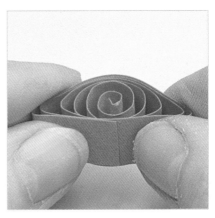

6 Take the narrower terracotta strip and make it into a Closed Loose Coil. Press it into a flattish 'D' shape.

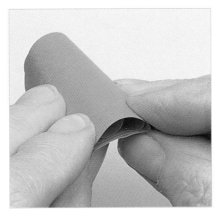

7 Do the same with the wider terracotta strip. Press the 'D' shape firmly on one side of the coil but rather less at the other. This creates more of a flowerpot shape.

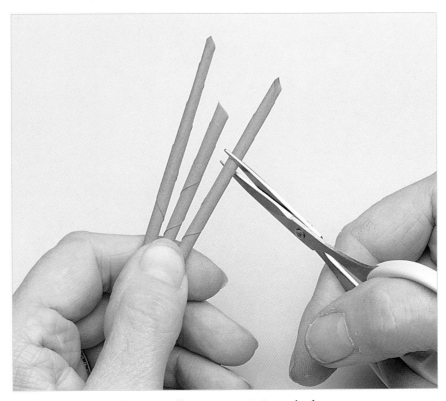

8 Each flower stalk is a spill (see page 26) made from a green square. Reduce the length of one stalk by 2cm (¾in) and another one by 3cm (1¼in) by snipping with sharp scissors.

9 Arrange the plant pot, flower stalks and flowers on your background card and glue down. Make a few Wheatear and Open Coils in green for foliage growing around the pot.

10 The leaves are made with the Alternate Side Looping technique. Use the leaf patterns on page 79. They look best made from 2mm or 1.5mm (¹/₁₆in) wide strips.

The finished Sunflowers project
Size: 10.5 x 21cm (4 x 8¼in)

Thistle

Height: 200mm (8in)

Generally speaking, I am not comfortable with symmetry, but some designs, like this, seem to ask for it. The super spiky thistle leaves were great fun to do in Alternate Side Looping, and the flower itself could not be better portrayed than with a finely fringed purple and mauve Pom-pom with occasional yellow tips.

Candle in Holder

Height: 330mm (13in)

Since they are strong and durable, you can used Fringed Flowers to make all kinds of decorations, just as you might use dried flowers. I made this candle holder from lots of very wide strips, big enough to support a full-sized candle. Then I covered them with a decoration of Fringed Flowers in Autumn colours. Because of the fire risk I made a paper candle to go with the holder instead of using the real thing.

Crimping, Zig-zagging and Tendrils

These traditional techniques were usually, though not always, used on antique quillings as borders. They were popular with our quilling ancestors, who used them to define the edges of their tea caddy panels or decorative plaques. We now find their handiwork inspirational. Close inspection often reveals just how the techniques were achieved, sometimes by hand, sometimes with the help of cogs. We can try to copy them or make our own devices to recreate them, putting them to traditional and modern uses.

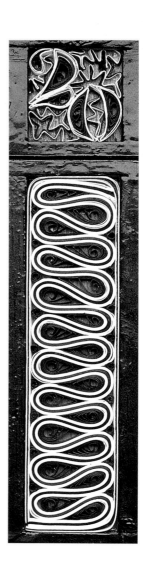

I decided to make this modern version of a Georgian tea caddy in black and white only. There are many antiques around featuring Crimping, Zig-zagging and Tendrils for me to study, so these techniques feature strongly in this piece.

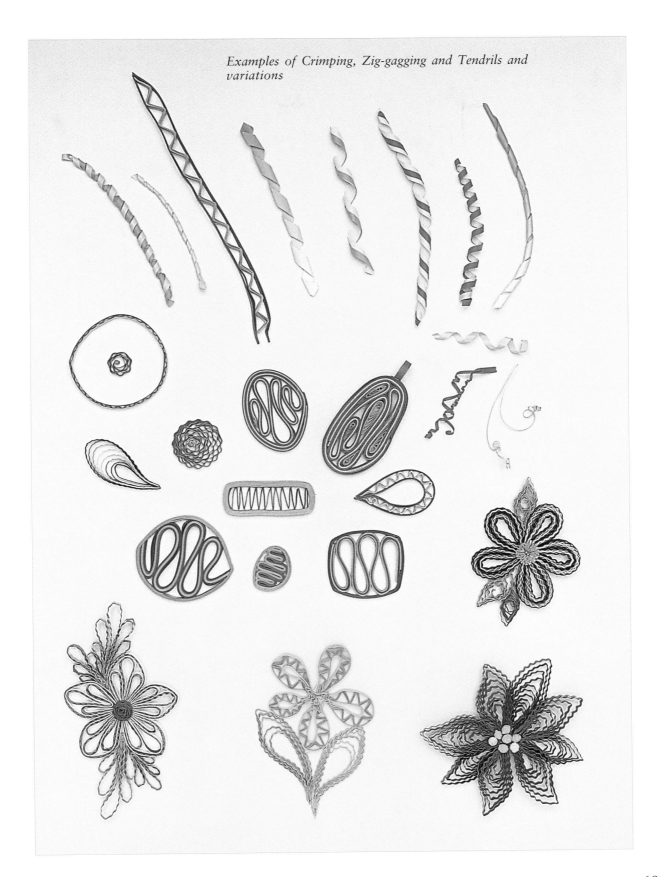

Examples of Crimping, Zig-gagging and Tendrils and variations

Techniques

Crimping and Zig-zagging are two versions of a very similar thing. I generally use the word 'Crimping' where a strip has been given a soft, wavy appearance and 'Zig-zagging' if the result is a series of angular, concertina-like folds. The gentle wave of Crimping is achieved by leading a paper strip between interlocking cogs. Different sized cogs will produce varied Crimping. Zig-zagging is usually done by hand so that you are not so much controlled by the size of cogs you can find, but you will need more practice.

Tendrils may also be made, with a little practice, in your fingers only, but where a Tendril with a regular, even appearance is required, quillers usually find a dowel of some kind helpful.

1 Crimped strips are produced by running a strip between cogs, as with this Crimping machine.

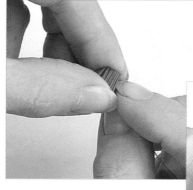

2 Zig-zagging can be achieved by bending a strip backwards and forwards between finger and thumb.

3 Perhaps an easier way to do short lengths of Zig-zagging is to take a wide strip of paper, about 4cm by up to 8cm (1½in x 3in), and fold it backwards and forwards, rather as you would to make a fan.

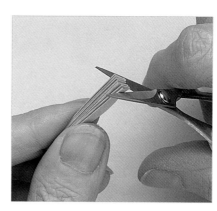

4 Now you can cut through the fan, while it is still folded, to the width required.

5 Rolling a Crimped length or, better still, two Crimped lengths together, creates an interesting effect.

6 If you attempt to roll a Zig-zagged strip, it will often turn obligingly into a star.

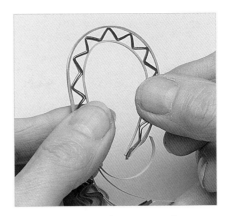

7 Crimping and Zig-zagging can be rather fragile so you can sandwich them between straight strips. This example shows five strips Zig-zagged together and five each side for a bolder appearance.

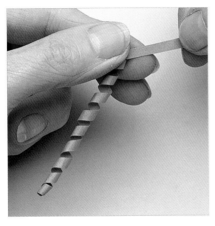

8 Tendrils can be made in your fingers. Curl over the strip end and then roll between finger and thumb but move the strip along as you go.

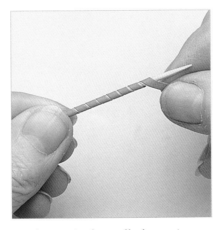

9 Alternatively, roll the strip, helter-skelterlike along a cocktail stick, corsage pin or other dowel.

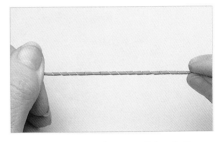

10 You can tighten a Tendril by taking it off the dowel and then stretching and twisting the whole length between your fingers.

Earrings

Jewellery can also be made from quilling. Before fixing the findings, treat the quilling with spray varnish to strengthen and protect it.

Preservation

On my bedroom wall, I have quillings, lovingly kept, which were made by my children about twenty years ago. Occasionally, I blow or flick the dust off them and they remain in fairly good condition, though slightly discoloured because they have been given no protection of any kind. As I am sure you know, paper which is left uncovered or unprotected will, over the course of time, discolour, deteriorate and, finally, decay.

In order to keep your quillings in perfect condition, you really do need to cover the paper in some way. Our ancestors often took advantage of glass, when it was available, and mounted their quillings inside box frames, which allow for the three-dimensional quality of quilling by providing adequate space between the background and the glass. Modern quillers often use this idea too, and a good variety of box frames is available.

You can also create your own box frame by converting a normal picture frame. Square or rectangular wooden doweling or strong card will hold the back away from the glass to the depth you require. Free-standing quillings, too, are often placed under glass domes or boxes, which provide the perfect protection.

We modern quillers also have another form of protection at our disposal. This is varnish in the form of aerosol spray. Clear, high gloss is really the best. Make sure you read the instructions very carefully before you begin. Apply several light coats, allowing each to dry before continuing. Too much at once may cause coils to unroll. Free-standing quillings can benefit greatly from a few light coats, and quillings on a suitable background will not only be protected but their colour will be enhanced. Perfect backgrounds for spraying are wood, hessian or cork but you could test any which seem appropriate before spray varnishing your complete mounted piece.

All quillings, protected or not, should really be kept away from strong, direct sunlight.

In fact, the vast majority of quilling is not given any kind of permanent protection, because it is made into greetings cards. We have to provide these with plenty of padding, usually in the form of bubble wrap, so that they are not crushed in the post. If they arrive intact, they will survive for many years even without protective measures. However, we quillers often think we have

Opposite

Unprotected quillings have a surprisingly long life, provided they are kept out of direct sunlight. However, for greater protection put them behind glass in a box frame, coat them with spray varnish or cover them with bubble wrap.

made a greetings card, only to discover that it has actually
become a picture. The recipient has appreciated the workmanship
and the thought behind it so much that they have mounted it in a
little box frame to be permanently on view.

Patterns

Pattern for the Art Nouveau Iris project on page 16

The second layer

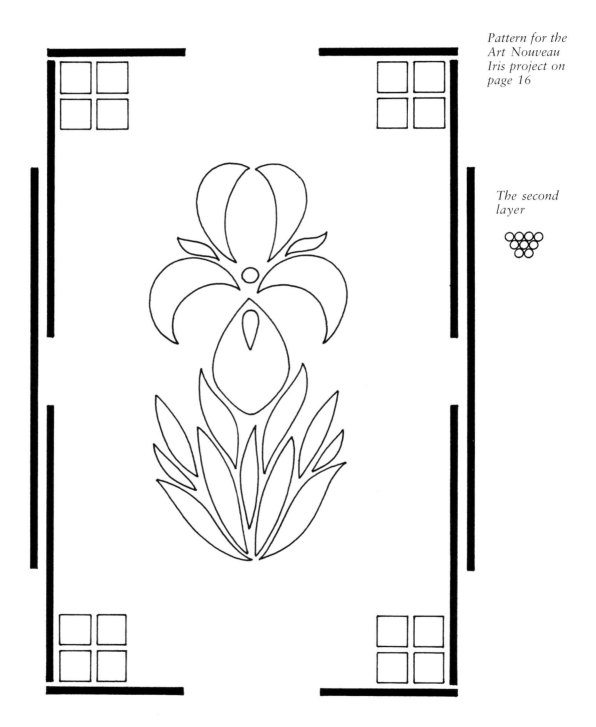

74

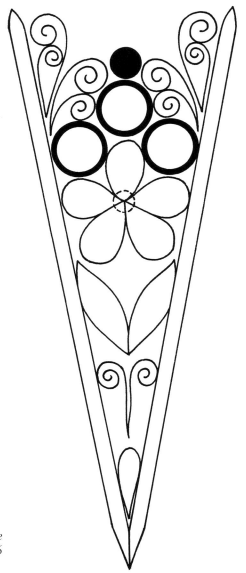

*The pattern for one section of the
Victorian Fan project on page 26*

The pattern for the Tulips project on page 34

The second layer

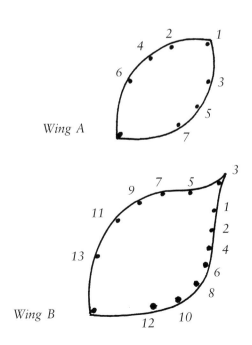

Wing A

Wing B

*The pattern for the Foxgloves
project on page 52*

The first layer

*The first and second
layers combined*

*The pattern for the Sunflowers
project on page 62*

The leaf patterns

Index